HOW TO INVEST IN FGN BONDS

A Beginner's Guide to Investing in Nigerian Government Bonds

Usiere Uko

First published in the United States as How to Invest in Bonds in 2017.

ISBN-13: 979-8-879-27344-1

SECOND EDITION

...To new frontiers, learning and growing

CONTENTS

INTRODUCTION

UNLOCKING THE POWER OF FGN BOND INVESTMENTS

Welcome to the world of bond investing, where financial opportunities abound for both seasoned investors and newcomers alike. In this comprehensive guide, we embark on a journey to demystify the intricacies of bond investment, empowering you to navigate the complexities of the financial market with confidence and clarity.

Bond investing serves as a cornerstone of financial strategies for nations, governments, and corporations seeking long-term funding. However, what many individuals overlook is that this avenue of investment is not exclusive to the elite; it is readily accessible to the general public.

I have met many people who are not aware that they can start investing in bonds today; either through a primary auction, secondary market, or through a money market fund. While many think they don't have enough funds, others are scared of leaving their money alone for so long. They wonder whether the investment won't outlive them. They view investing in bonds as 'tying down' their money. They are unaware of the fact that they can buy and sell bonds pretty much the same way you can buy and sell shares.

This guide is not just about steps to investing in bonds. It addresses the mindset required, the what, and the why.

Knowing the way is only half the story; understanding why and developing the ability to go the distance is what separates the doers from the talkers. It helps move you away from the paralysis by analysis mode to dipping your toes in the pool.

This guide is for people looking to build long-term financial security through investing in the Nigerian Government issued FGN Bonds (FGN - Federal Government of Nigeria). Investing in bonds is one way to achieve that. It focuses on buying bonds from the secondary market, primary auction, and how to sell your bond before maturity through the secondary market.

This beginner guide will not make you a bond trading expert. If you are ready to finally do it, let's go.

1: WHAT ARE BONDS?

Bonds, in straightforward terms, involve lending to nations, governments, and corporations. Issuing bonds is one of the ways governments or corporations borrow money from the general public, a group that includes individuals (including you), financial institutions, both local and foreign, and foreign governments.

The investor or holder of the bond is the lender, while the issuer of the bond is the borrower. When you purchase a bond, you are essentially lending money to a Government (Federal, State, Local Government Council, or Agency) or Corporation.

When you purchase a bond, the issuer promises to pay you a specified rate of interest (the coupon) during the life of the bond, in addition to repaying the face value of the bond at maturity. The borrower makes interest payments bi-annually (twice a year) in the form of a dividend warrant or directly to an account designated by you.

This means you receive payment every six months—six months after you bought the bond and every six months until the bond matures. The interest income becomes one of your sources of income which you can spend, save, or reinvest.

In Nigeria, Federal Government of Nigeria (FGN) bonds are issued by the Central Bank of Nigeria (CBN) on behalf of the Debt Management Office (DMO). The Government must pay the bondholder the principal and agreed-upon interest as and when due. When you buy FGN Bonds, you are lending to the FGN for an agreed duration.

The tenor or duration of the bond varies from about two years to 30 years. In the primary market (where you buy directly at an auction), the tenors on offer are two and three years for the Federal Savings Bond and five to 30 years for FGN Bonds.

In the secondary market (where investors sell previously issued bonds), you can find a wide range of available tenors (time to maturity) on an existing bond. For example, if an investor with a 5-year tenor bond holds it for three years and eight months before selling, you are buying a one year four months tenor bond.

Government bonds are considered the safest of all investments in the domestic debt market. Bonds are backed by the 'full faith and credit' of the Federal Government, being "charged upon the general assets of Nigeria". That means the Federal Government is borrowing using its assets as collateral. As such, bonds are classified as a risk-free debt instrument. This means if there is a default, the nation's assets can be seized to liquidate the debt. Bonds typically have no default risk, meaning governments always meet this debt obligation. The interest income earned from the bond is tax-exempt (interest-free).

The government issues bonds for reasons which include, but are not limited to:

- To finance government fiscal deficits

- To enhance the budgetary discipline of the Government

- To refinance maturing debt obligations of the Government

- To establish a benchmark yield curve, serving as a reference for pricing bonds issued by other bodies, especially private sector issuers.

- To develop and ensure liquidity in the domestic bond market

- To enhance and deepen the savings and investment opportunities

- To sustain the development of other segments of the Bond market

- To diversify government financing sources By having a thriving bonds market, the Government has a ready market to borrow from for long-term projects like infrastructure projects. The long tenor of bonds helps in long-term planning and projections.

The investing public purchases bonds in Nigeria through licensed Primary Dealer/Market Makers (PDMM). PDMMs are banks appointed by the DMO to act as authorized dealers in FGN bonds. The terminology may differ in other countries. You can find the current list on the website of the body responsible for issuing bonds in your country (in Nigeria, it is www.dmo.gov.ng). Chapter 5 shows the current list of PDMMs (updated August 1, 2018). Non-PDMM Banks and other financial institutions can bid for bonds for their clients through PDMMs.

All you need to do to invest in bonds through the primary market is to submit a bid for the auction by filling in the required form and funding your bid as needed. However, you need to understand how the whole process works.

In Nigeria, the minimum subscription for FGN Bonds is N50 Million with effect from March 6, 2017. However, you can purchase FGN Bonds for less through the secondary market.

To cater to the segment of the population that cannot afford the minimum bid amount of N50 Million, the Nigerian Government introduced the Federal Savings Bond which has a minimum subscription of N5,000 with multiples of N1,000 after that. The DMO appointed accredited stockbrokers as primary dealers.

However, for administrative reasons, most dealers segment their target market and set their minimum subscription amount ranging from N100,000 to N10 Million based on their niche. For a bid to be valid, an investor has to fund their account to cover the amount of the bid and commissions. A prospective investor has to locate a broker that works for them.

If you have challenges meeting up with the minimum amount required, you can invest in a money market fund which has bonds in its portfolio. Most brokers have such in-house funds. This way, you benefit from the higher returns with more flexible entry and exit as you are dealing directly with the broker instead of a third party.

There are different types of bonds.

SOVEREIGN BONDS (GOVERNMENT BONDS, E.G. FGN BONDS)

These bonds are issued by sovereign nations or governments, representing a direct lending arrangement between investors and a country, such as Nigeria, Kenya, or the US. When you purchase FGN bonds, for instance, you are essentially lending money to the Federal Government of Nigeria for a specified period. Governments typically issue bonds in their local denominations.

As mentioned earlier, the FGN Bond is considered the safest form of investment due to its backing by the 'full faith and credit' of the Government. The consequences of default are so significant that no nation contemplates it unless facing extreme circumstances like bankruptcy or wartime disruptions. Even in war situations, governments typically honor their debt obligations once hostilities cease.

SAVINGS BONDS (E.G. FGN SAVINGS BONDS)

Sovereign nations or governments also issue savings bonds, which are essentially sovereign bonds but with distinct terms and conditions as stipulated by the issuer.

Savings bonds are typically offered at a fixed coupon rate, simplifying the subscription process for investors who need not place bids but can directly apply for subscription.

In Nigeria, FGN-issued savings bonds have tenors of 2, 3, and 5 years and make interest payments quarterly. These bonds are issued monthly, with a subscription window usually open for five days. Announcements regarding subscription are disseminated through press releases in major national newspapers.

SPECIAL PURPOSE BONDS

Special Purpose bonds are issued to raise funds for specific projects, such as infrastructure developments like highways or railways, or for debt settlement purposes. The terms and conditions for these bonds are outlined in the offer document, and the government may reserve the right to liquidate them before maturity under certain circumstances.

MUNICIPAL BONDS (STATE AND LOCAL GOVERNMENT COUNCILS)

Municipal bonds are issued by state governments or local government councils, operating similarly to sovereign bonds but with a lower authority as the issuer.

These bonds are typically guaranteed by the Federal Government, and in Nigeria, they are backed by an Irrevocable Standing Payment Order (ISPO) ensuring deductions from the state's revenue share for bond repayment.

GOVERNMENT AGENCY BONDS

Government agency bonds are issued by government agencies to finance specific projects. While they do not carry the full faith and credit of the Government, they are still highly regarded by investors due to the backing of a government entity.

CORPORATE BONDS

Corporate bonds are debt securities issued by private or public companies, often offering higher interest rates than government bonds due to perceived higher risk. Interest income from corporate bonds is typically taxable unless tax exemptions are granted by the Government. Unlike stocks, corporate bonds do not confer ownership interest in the issuing corporation, though some can be converted to equity under certain conditions, known as convertible bonds.

EUROBONDS

Sovereign governments issue Eurobonds for subscription by foreign investors and citizens residing abroad. Eurobonds are typically denominated in a currency other than the issuing country's home currency, and domestic investors can access them through the secondary market. Eurobonds offer attractiveness to investors due to their small par values, high liquidity, and ability to serve as a hedge against inflation compared to local currencies. Mutual and money market funds also trade Eurobonds, providing local investors with access to foreign currency-denominated investments.

Nigerian Eurobonds are predominantly denominated in US dollars.

***

The primary purpose of investing in bonds is to gain access to long-term stable income in the form of interest or coupon payments. There are different types of coupons, depending on the bond, usually indicated in the bond prospectus. These types include:

Coupon Bond: This is the most common type, covered in this guide. It obligates the issuer to make fixed interest payments, called coupon payments, over the life of the bond, and to repay the principal (the bond's face or par value) at maturity. The coupon rate remains constant throughout the lifespan of the bond.

Floating Rate Bond: The coupon rate for this bond is anchored on another rate that is variable, either plus or minus. This means the coupon rate varies during the life of the bond in response to changes in the anchor rate. In Nigeria, such bonds are anchored on the Nigeria Inter-Bank Offered Rate (NIBOR), which is the annualized rate at which banks borrow from each other. This bond is designed to minimize the holder's interest rate risk, as the interest rate that the borrower pays is adjusted periodically depending on market conditions.

Zero-Coupon Bonds: A Zero-coupon bond carries no coupon and must provide all its return in the form of price appreciation at maturity. This bond is sold at a discounted price and does not make periodic interest payments. They are often bonds that have been stripped of their coupons by a financial institution and then repackaged as zero-coupon bonds. Zero-coupon bonds tend to fluctuate in price much more than coupon bonds.

Bond certificates can be either electronic or printed, although printed certificates are being phased out. In Nigeria, bonds are domiciled electronically at the Central Securities Clearing System (CSCS) as a Central Depository, Clearing, and Settlement of transactions in the Nigerian Capital Market. This is facilitated through a stockbroker, meaning that holders of bonds can be verified at the CSCS. The investor can also opt to have her bond (bought at the secondary market) domiciled with a Custodian.

Bonds are listed on the stock exchange and are tradable on the floor of the Exchange (a part of the secondary market) the same way stocks are. This means you can sell your bond on the floor of the Exchange through a stockbroker. In the following chapters, I will take you through a step-by-step process of investing in bonds either through the primary market or secondary market, and liquidating before maturity through the secondary market.

2: BENEFITS OF FGN BONDS INVESTING

I n this chapter, we'll delve into the numerous benefits of investing in FGN bonds, shedding light on why it's a smart move for both seasoned investors and those just starting their financial journey.

STABILITY AND SECURITY

FGN bonds offer stability and security, making them an attractive option for conservative investors. Backed by the Nigerian government, these bonds offer a virtually risk-free investment opportunity. Unlike stocks, which can be volatile and subject to market fluctuations, FGN bonds provide a steady stream of income with minimal risk. This stability is particularly appealing for investors looking to preserve their capital while still earning a reliable return.

GUARANTEED RETURNS

One of the key benefits of investing in FGN bonds is the guaranteed returns they offer. When you purchase a bond, you know exactly how much interest you will receive and when you will receive it. This predictability makes it easier to plan your finances and achieve your long-term goals. Whether you're saving for retirement, funding your children's education, or building an emergency fund, FGN bonds provide a reliable source of income that you can count on.

FIXED INCOME STREAM

FGN bonds offer a fixed income stream, meaning you receive regular interest payments at predetermined intervals. This fixed income can provide stability and security, especially during times of economic uncertainty. Whether the market is up or down, you can rely on your FGN bonds to generate steady cash flow, helping you meet your financial obligations and maintain your standard of living.

DIVERSIFICATION

Diversification is a cornerstone of sound investment strategy, and FGN bonds can play a valuable role in diversifying your portfolio. By adding bonds to your investment mix, you can reduce overall risk and enhance long-term returns. FGN bonds often have low correlation with other asset classes, such as stocks and real estate, making them an effective way to spread risk and protect your portfolio against market downturns.

TAX ADVANTAGES

In addition to their stability and predictability, FGN bonds offer tax advantages that can help you maximize your investment returns. Interest income from FGN bonds is exempt from state and local taxes, providing a tax-efficient way to grow your wealth. By taking advantage of these tax benefits, you can keep more of your investment earnings and accelerate your journey towards financial independence.

ACCESSIBILITY

Investing in FGN bonds is accessible to investors of all levels, from seasoned professionals to beginners. With a wide range of bond options available, you can tailor your investment strategy to suit your individual needs and preferences. Whether you prefer short-term or long-term bonds, fixed or floating rates, there's an FGN bond that's right for you. Plus, with low minimum investment requirements, you can start investing in FGN bonds with as little as N5,000 for FGN Savings Bonds, making it easy to get started on your financial journey.

Investing in FGN bonds offers a host of benefits, including stability, guaranteed returns, fixed income stream, diversification, tax advantages, and accessibility. Whether you're looking to generate reliable income, or build wealth over time, FGN bonds provide a solid foundation for achieving your financial goals.

3: HOW SAFE ARE FGN BONDS?

Any time you lend money, you run the risk of not getting it back; this is known as credit risk. You may have experienced lending to a friend in need and never seeing the money again. Investing in bonds means lending to the Government, which generally cannot afford to default. It typically allocates funds for debt obligations, including bonds, in its annual budget. A default drastically lowers the Government's credit rating and can scare away investors and creditors, both domestic and foreign.

Consequently, future bonds issued by the same government may be considered useless or junk bonds. Consequently, the Government seeks funds from other sources to redeem previous bonds, including issuing new ones.

The security lies in the fact that bonds issued by the Government carry the full faith and credit of the Government. A default erodes this faith, and with it, the confidence of investors to invest in future bonds. No government wants to be in such a situation, except under extreme financial distress or during a full-scale war when a fully functional government is absent.

Government-issued bonds are considered the safest investment instruments, with virtually no default risk as the Government always gives priority to bond subscribers in debt repayments.

Apart from the low credit risk, another risk factor for some class of bonds (those with call options) is that the issuer can repay before the maturity date. That means if you had planned your future cash flow based on getting fixed interest income from your 20-year tenor bond, and the issuer redeems the bond before 20 years, you are back in the market earlier than planned. The going coupon rate at this time may not align with your original plan. This is known as prepayment risk, and the prospectus will indicate whether a bond is callable.

Another risk, common to all types of investing, is inflation risk, which becomes an issue due to the relatively long tenor of the investment. If you hold the bond until maturity, the inflation rate may increase during its tenor.

Inflation also impacts bond prices in the secondary market, producing higher interest rates and resulting in a higher discount rate, thereby decreasing a bond's price. Related to this is interest rate risk; as coupon rates drop, prices of previously issued bonds increase. These fluctuations are not relevant if you hold your bond to maturity, as discussed in more detail when we look at liquidating your bond before maturity through the secondary market.

Inflation risk, credit risk, and prepayment risk are all considered in the pricing of bonds; the more the risk, the higher the yield. Investors demand higher yields for longer maturities, as the longer you tie your money up in a bond, the more you are exposed to these risks. That means longer-tenor bonds attract higher interest rates, while shorter tenor bonds attract lower rates. The higher rate compensates for future uncertainties due to the relatively longer tenor.

FGN Bonds have an active secondary market through the stock market, over the counter (OTC) through PDMMs, and trading platforms like Financial Markets Dealers Quotes (FMDQ) in Nigeria, where prices fluctuate based on supply and demand forces. Dealers provide buying and selling prices (two-way quotes) to ensure transparency.

The spread, which is the difference between the selling price and bid price, gives an indication of liquidity in the market. A wide spread indicates low liquidity, while a narrow spread indicates high liquidity. This also indicates how soon you can sell your bonds if you desire to liquidate prematurely. It is possible to lose some money as a seller in the secondary market if bond prices drop.

This guide is for beginners and individuals seeking to build financial security through investing in bonds. Hence, the focus will be on investing in the primary market and holding to maturity. However, since the minimum subscription for the primary market in Nigeria is above N50 million, Chapter 6 will detail how to buy bonds to achieve higher returns than other money market instruments.

Investing in bonds offers several advantages, including regular, predictable income, tax-free status, stability compared to the stock market, potential appreciation, and acceptance as collateral for loans. Bonds also yield higher interest rates than savings accounts and most money market instruments.

The bonds market is very active, and you need to have a strategy to achieve your financial goals. Your overall financial goal should drive your actions in the bonds market, not current market conditions.

In the next chapter, we address the question of why we invest in bonds.

4: WHY INVEST IN FGN BONDS?

Investing in bonds should be part of an overall strategy to achieve financial independence. To accomplish that, you need to know how to build a solid financial structure to deliver the results you desire. Financial independence means having a guaranteed regular income to support your lifestyle without having to work.

Achieving financial independence means different things to different people in terms of how much you need. Whatever figure works for you, financial independence means that if you lose your primary source of income (wages, pensions, proceeds from the business), your life goes on as usual without having to seek a bailout.

To build a solid or stable financial structure, you need to understand what it is and how to go about building one that works for you.

To have a stable financial structure, you need a proper foundation. That foundation is financial security. This security does not come from your job or your business; it comes from earning enough from other guaranteed (relatively risk-free) income sources to maintain your lifestyle if you lose your job or your business goes belly up. That means your life is independent of earned income.

It is on the foundation of financial security that you build other elements. In my previous books, "***Practical Steps to Financial***

Freedom & Independence" and *"Your Ultimate Money Makeover,"* I dedicated some time to explaining the concept of asset allocation as a tool for building a solid financial foundation. Here, I'll provide a brief recap.

You need to build the right financial structure to achieve financial stability through the ups and downs of any economic cycle. This financial structure is built on having your money work for you. Your job is to convert a part of your earned income (income you work for) into passive income (that you don't work for) - building a structure whereby money works for you so that you eventually don't have to work for money anymore, but for love.

Whatever you are doing will come to an end someday. Your job will not last forever. You will leave it one way or the other, including mandatory retirement at a certain age. The marketplace is continuously evolving. Market trends, technology, etc., will someday render your business model irrelevant. The economy goes up and down, and this has an impact on your business. You need to build a financial support structure, a financial portfolio that will give you financial stability.

Two plans make up this financial structure:

FINANCIAL SECURITY PLAN

This plan is to make your family financially secure in terms of being able to sustain your current standard of living. It is not to make you rich. Investments under this plan are fixed-income investments whereby the returns are guaranteed, and risk is almost zero. Investments in this plan include money market investments like fixed deposits, treasury bills, etc. Bonds are also included in this plan.

FINANCIAL GROWTH PLAN

This plan is to enable you to grow financially; essentially increase your net worth and raise your standard of living if you so desire. This plan is to make you comfortable. Returns under this plan are potentially higher than under the financial security plan. The risks are also higher (higher risk, higher reward). You can make a lot of money and can lose a lot of money if you don't know what you are doing. Investments under this plan include stocks, real estate, forex trading, etc.; investments that appreciate.

For those who desire to become rich, there is a third plan:

FINANCIAL ABUNDANCE PLAN

This plan is to make you rich, a millionaire, multi-millionaire, billionaire (depending on your financial goals), whereby you can afford anything you want. Investments under this plan, as you may have rightly guessed, are high risk and high reward. You can become very rich if it goes well, and you may end up in debt if it goes wrong. Such investments include investing in startups; that includes known success stories like Apple, Facebook, Twitter, Google, Linkedin, WhatsApp, YouTube, Instagram, etc. There is also another list – those that did not make it. Many consider this a part of the financial growth plan.

***

So how do you tie all this together to build a solid financial structure? The answer is asset allocation.

ASSET ALLOCATION

You are working hard, saving before spending, and using your savings to invest. Where do you put the money?

If you have a regular income, you need to start building the plans or portfolios, starting from the foundation, which is the financial security plan where the risk is virtually zero.

When you are just starting, you don't know much and are probably afraid of losing your hard-earned money. Every building begins from the foundation. Building a financial security plan is the starting point, and bonds are a valuable addition to your financial security plan.

However, you need to understand that you need to build one on top of the other. Rather than building your financial security today, demolish tomorrow which is what most people do. They start building their security plan together, find a riskier investment elsewhere, so they liquidate their safe investment for a risky one. That also includes lending to a friend with an untested business idea. Many end up badly, stuff that keeps legal reality shows like Judge Judy going season after season.

I often use football to illustrate asset allocation. The next figure shows a conventional 4-4-2 formation.

The goalkeeper (1) and the defenders (2 – 5) make up the DEFENSE which represents the FINANCIAL SECURITY PLAN.

The midfielders (6 – 9) and attackers (10, 11) make up the ATTACK which represents the FINANCIAL GROWTH PLAN.

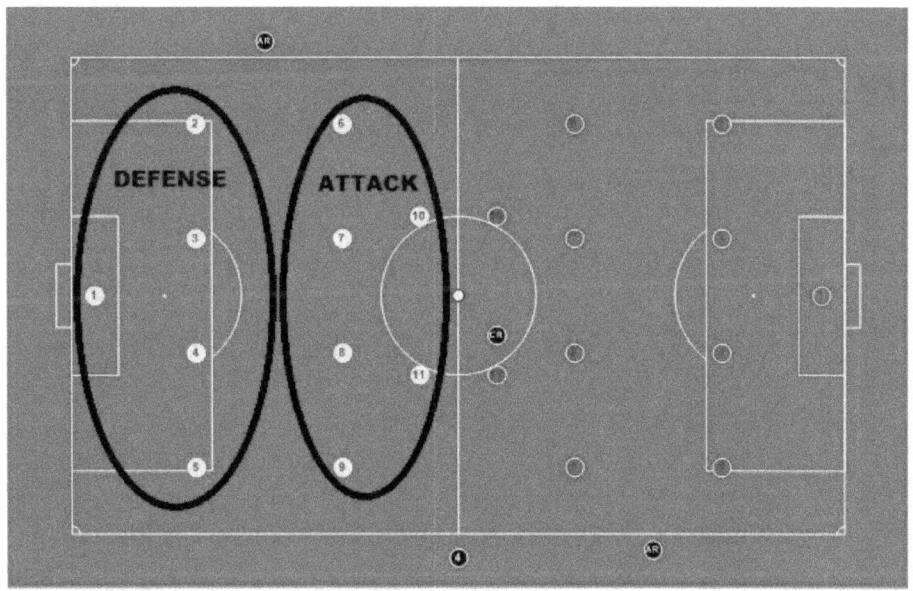

Football field showing players in a 4-4-2 soccer formation

You need both the defense and attack to win the game. You don't collapse the defense simply because you are desperate to score a goal. If you do that, you expose your back and leave your net open if the opponent counterattacks, which life often does.

With this understanding, let's explore in detail the business of buying bonds at a primary auction.

5: HOW FGN BONDS PRIMARY AUCTION WORKS

There are two types of FGN Bonds available to investors in the Nigerian primary bonds market – new issues and reopened bonds. New issues are fresh bonds introduced to the market while reopened bonds are previously issued bonds being reissued via an auction to new investors.

The Debt Management Office (DMO) routinely makes available reopened bonds available to the investing public through an auction. This chapter deals with reopened bonds.

The DMO usually issues a quarterly bonds issuance calendar. The calendar shows auction dates, the name of the bond, offered coupon rates, term to maturity, range of amount on offer, and original tenor.

DEFINITION OF TERMS

Bond name: The bond name shows the coupon rate, issuer name, and maturity date.

Re-opening: In a bond re-opening, the issuer issues additional amounts of a previously issued bond. The re-opened bond has the same maturity date and coupon interest rate, but with a different issue date and usually a different purchase price (determined through an auction).

Term to maturity: Time till maturity; applicable to previously issued bonds.

Range of amount on offer: This is the range of the amount on offer (in Billions of Naira). The actual amount sold is determined at the close of the auction. The exact figure allocated will fall within this range.

Original tenor: This is the tenor at the first issue of the bond.

DEBT MANAGEMENT OFFICE
NIGERIA

FGN BONDS ISSUANCE CALENDAR FOR Q1, 2017

Auction Dates	Particulars				
18-Jan	Bond Name	14.50% FGN JUL 2021 (Re-opening)	12.50% FGN JAN 2026 (Re-opening)		12.40% FGN MAR 2036 (Re-opening)
	Term-To-Maturity	4 Years, 6 Months	8 Years, 11 Months		19 Years, 2 Months
	Range of Amount on Offer (N' bil)	35 - 45	45 - 55		35 - 45
	Original Tenor	5-Year	10-Year		20-Year
15-Feb	Bond Name	14.50% FGN JUL 2021 (Re-opening)	12.50% FGN JAN 2026 (Re-opening)		12.40% FGN MAR 2036 (Re-opening)
	Term-To-Maturity	4 Years, 5 Months	9 Years, 1 Month		19 Years, 1 Month
	Range of Amount on Offer (N' bil)	40-50	40-50		40-50
	Original Tenor	5-Year	10-Year		20-Year
15-Mar	Bond Name	14.50% FGN JUL 2021 (Re-opening)		FGN MAR 2027 (New Issue)	12.40% FGN MAR 2036 (Re-opening)
	Term-To-Maturity	4 Years, 4 Months		10 Years	19 Years
	Range of Amount on Offer (N' bil)	35 - 45		45-55	25 - 35
	Original Tenor	5-Year		10-Year	20-Year

DMO first quarter 2017 Bonds issuance calendar

The figure shows the actual issue program for the first quarter of 2017. The header (Bond Name) indicates the names of previously issued bonds on offer while the next line (Time to Maturity) indicates time left on the bond.

The CBN conducts a monthly auction on behalf of the DMO, typically on Wednesdays. It sells FGN bonds via an auction system where investors quote their bid rates and the amount of bonds requested. These previously issued bonds have been trading in the bonds market for a while hence are not at par value.

PDMMs are required to submit tenders for bonds before 1.30 pm on the auction date. Every valid bid must be funded, which means funds for the purchase of bonds must be in the custody of the broker.

At the close of each auction, successful bids are selected. These are bids with rates that fall within the range of the amount offered for bid, starting from the lowest bid. Bids above the cut-off rate are unsuccessful.

The marginal rate is calculated based on the winning bids. The CBN allocates Bonds to investors with winning bids at the marginal rate. That is different from Treasury Bills, where allocation is based on individual bid rates.

Below is an actual result of the January 18, 2017, primary auction for FGN Bonds. It shows the auction date, tenor and maturity date, account offered, total subscription received, total successful subscriptions, the range of submitted bid rates, the range of successful bid rates, and the marginal rate.

DEBT MANAGEMENT OFFICE
NIGERIA

The Presidency
NDIC Building (1ᵗ Floor), Plot 447/448, Constitution Avenue, Central Business District, PMB 532, Garki, Abuja
Tel: +2348110000881
Website: http//www.dmo.gov.ng

Auction Result for the 14.50% FGN JUL 2021 (Re-opening), 12.50% FGN JAN 2026 (Re-opening) & 12.40% FGN MAR 2036 (Re-opening)

	14.50% FGN JUL 2021	12.50% FGN JAN 2026	12.40% FGN MAR 2036
Auction Date:	January 18, 2017	January 18, 2017	January 18, 2017
Settlement Date:	January 20, 2017	January 20, 2017	January 20, 2017
Maturity Date:	July 15, 2021	January 22, 2026	March 18, 2036
Tenors:	5-Year	10-Year	20-Year
Term-To-Maturity:	4 Years, 6 Months	9 Years	19 Years, 2 Months
Amount Offered:	₦40.00 billion	₦50.00 billion	₦40.00 billion
Total Bids:	51	78	121
Successful Bids:	47	73	113
Subscription:	₦39.15 billion	₦83.00 billion	₦112.90 billion
Amount Allotted:	₦34.95 billion	₦74.90 billion	₦105.10 billion
Range of Bids:	15.0000% - 17.2590%	16.0000% - 18.0000%	14.0000% - 18.0000%
Marginal Rates:	16.8990%	16.9945%	16.9920%

Successful bids for the 14.50% FGN JUL 2021, 12.50% FGN JAN 2026 and 12.40% FGN MAR 2036 were allotted at the Marginal Rates of 16.8990%, 16.9945% and 16.9920%, respectively. However, the original coupon rates of 14.50% for the 14.50% FGN JUL 2021, 12.50% for the 12.50% FGN JAN 2026, and 12.40 for the 12.40% FGN MAR 2036 will be maintained.

Results of the DMO FGN Bonds auction held January 18, 2017

Auction results are transmitted to PDMMs the next day (Thursday). Afterward, brokers send allotment letters to successful bidders.

Coupon payments are made based on the coupon rate, not the marginal rate.

In the results above, the marginal rate is higher than the coupon rate. That means the investor is buying the bond at a discount (below N100 per unit). When the marginal rate is lower than the coupon rate, the investor is purchasing the bond at a premium (above N100 per unit).

The actual calculations are not relevant at this stage. What you need to know is that when the marginal rate is higher than the coupon rate, the buyer buys at a discount. The opposite is true when the marginal rate is lower than the coupon rate; the buyer pays a premium.

Let's assume you placed a bid for N55 million of the 14.50% FGN Jul 2021 bond at 16%, which falls within the bid range of 15.00% - 17.259%; that means your bid was successful.

Your investment summary will look something like this:

Bond Type	14.5% FGN JUL 2021
Settlement date	20-Jan-17
Maturity	15-Jul-21
Coupon	14.5000%
Yield (input)	16.8990%
Frequency	2
Basis	1
Last coupon payment	15-Jul-17
Next coupon payment	15-Jan-18
Clean Price (solve)	92.64
Accrued interest	X.XXX
Dirty Price	X.XXX
Nominal Amount	55,000,000.00
Cash Amount	50,962,000.00

I have removed some terms to keep it simple. The formula is complicated and unnecessary at this level. There are online calculators you can use to calculate the clean price if you are interested. One such calculator is available at https://www.free-online-calculator-use.com/bond-value-calculator.html.

To interpret the table, you will be paying N92.64 per unit for an N100 per unit bond (in total, N50,962,000 for an N55,000,000 bond – a discount of N4,038,000).

The clean price is the current market value of the bond, while the dirty price refers to the actual amount you pay the bondholder, which factors in accrued interest (since the last coupon payment) on the bond.

Your annual interest is 14.50% of N55,000,000, which is N7,975,000. The CBN will pay you N3,987,500 every July 20 and January 20 until the maturity date of July 15, 2021. Upon maturity, you will receive the full nominal amount of N55,000,000.

As a source of income, you can build up your savings to a level where interest payments cover your monthly expenses (more on this in later). That would mean each coupon payment you receive is enough to cover six months' living expenses. If you are saving towards your children's school fees, you can have a dedicated money market account (e.g., fixed deposits) where your bi-annual interest goes to work pending the time tuition fees are due (if the child is still in school). If it is for future tuition, you can use this money market account to build up the accrued interest to the level where you can buy another bond to add to your children's school fees portfolio.

AT WHAT RATE SHOULD YOU BID?

You can use the range of bid rates of the last auction as a guide.

Your broker can advise if they expect the rates to go up or down based on market fundamentals. Go with a bid rate you are comfortable with, as bidding too low to win will help drag down the marginal rate computation, which comes back to bite you.

You need to have an idea of what range of bid rates works for you within the context of your financial plan and projected future cash flows. You need to know where your bottom is, and rather lose the bid than accept a rate that doesn't work for you.

If your bid was not successful, you have the option of waiting for the next primary auction (moving the funds into a money market instrument in the interim) or purchasing in the secondary market.

6: HOW TO PLACE A BID IN AN FGN BOND PRIMARY AUCTION

Placing a bid in the FGN bonds primary auction (re-opening) is as simple and straightforward as investing in the money market. All you need to do is open an account with a PDMM or broker and fund your account to the required minimum amount to carry out transactions.

The first step is to decide with whom you want to deal and pay them a fact-finding visit (some will gladly come to you) or schedule a call. The broker will be more than willing to answer any questions you may have and assist in any way they can.

Below is the list of licensed PDMMs by the DMO as of November 24, 2023.

1. Access Bank Plc
2. Citibank Nigeria Ltd
3. Coronation Merchant Bank Ltd
4. Ecobank Nigeria Ltd
5. FBNQuest Merchant Bank Ltd
6. First Bank of Nigeria Ltd
7. First City Monument Bank Ltd
8. FSDH Merchant Bank Ltd
9. Guaranty Trust Bank Ltd
10. Rand Merchant Bank Nigeria Ltd
11. Stanbic IBTC Bank Plc
12. Standard Chartered Bank Nigeria Ltd
13. United Bank for Africa Plc

14. Zenith Bank Plc

If your bank is not on the list, you can still invest in bonds through your bank, stockbroker, or finance/investment house. They usually trade in bonds via PDMMs.

Do your due diligence and decide which broker to use. Your investment is safe with whichever broker you choose—FGN Bonds are domiciled with licensed custodians or the CSCS, not brokers. What you are looking for is integrity, good service, and support.

The CBN remits coupon payments directly to your indicated bank account, including the nominal value of the bond at redemption. If your broker goes out of business, there are processes to enable you to transfer to another broker.

Investing in bonds is almost risk-free, so there is no point in overthinking it. If you have made the decision to invest in FGN Bonds, simply go to your bank or finance house and get the process started.

On the next page is the actual application form. Every investor is required to fill out this form themselves, not by proxy. If you do not have a signature, a thumbprint is acceptable.

Filling out the form is simple and straightforward.

In Part A of the form, you are to indicate how much you want to invest (the minimum subscription for FGN bonds is N50,001,000.00, and multiples of N1,000 after that). You are also required to state the amount in words below.

For a new issue, the amount indicated is what you will pay if the bid is successful.

For a re-opening, you will need to indicate your bid rate. You will also need your broker to calculate the cash amount required to fund your bid if the expected marginal rate is lower than the coupon rate (i.e., you are buying at a premium). This allows you to know the actual capital outlay for your bid before you proceed.

To:
Director,
Financial Markets Department,
Central Bank of Nigeria,
Abuja.

No: ☐☐☐☐☐☐
Official use only

DEBT MANAGEMENT OFFICE
NIGERIA

TENDER FOR FEDERAL GOVERNMENT OF NIGERIA BONDS

Applications must be made in accordance with the instructions set out on the back of this application form. Care must be taken to follow these instructions as applications that do not comply with the instructions may be rejected. If you are in any doubt, please consult your stockbroker, Banker, Solicitor, or any professional adviser for guidance.

In response to the advertisement in both print and electronic media, I/We hereby offer my/our tender for the auction of the

_____
(Full title of Bond)

A

Guide to Applications		Value of Bonds Applied For N	Bid Interest Rate (%)	Allotment Preference (Please Tick X)		E-allotment Details Applicant CSCS A/C No.
				Certificate	Electronic	
Minimum Value	N 10,000					
Multiples therefore	N 1,000					

B

Amount in Words	

1 Individual Applicants (to be completed in block letters)

Full Name(Surname first)..
(State titles if any e.g Mr.,Mrs., Miss)

Occupation:...........................Phone No...............

Next of Kin..

Contact Address:..

Full Postal Address..

E-mail Address:..

Name of Bank/Branch..

Bank Account No:........................Sort Code:...............
(For interest payment purpose)

Usual Signature........................Date...............

Residency classification of Applicant (tick the appropriate box)
Resident ☐   Non-Resident ☐
(Residency classification of Applicant must be indicated)

2 Joint Applicants (to be completed in block letters)

Full Name(Surname first)..
(State titles if any e.g Mr.,Mrs., Miss)

Occupation:...........................Phone No...............

Next of Kin..

Contact Address:..

Full Postal Address..

E-mail Address:..

Name of Bank/Branch..

Bank Account No:........................Sort Code:...............
(For interest payment purpose)

Usual Signature........................Date...............

Residency classification of Applicant (tick the appropriate box)
Resident ☐   Non-Resident ☐
(Residency classification of Applicant must be indicated)

3 Corporate Applicants (to be completed in block letters)

Company's Name:..

Type of Business:..

Contact Address:..

Full Postal Address:..

E-mail Address:..

Contact Person:........................Telephone No...............

Signature:........................Signature...............

Name of Bank/Branch..

Bank Account No........................Sort Code...............
(For interest payment purpose)

Residency classification of Applicant (tick the appropriate Box)
Resident ☐   Non-Resident ☐
(Residency classification of Applicant must be indicated)

Please affix company seal and RC Number

C
Thumb print of Illiterate applicant

Witness: I........................have
given detailed explanation to this applicant in the language understood by him and consequently the applicant has a clear understanding of the transaction he has entered into.

Signature:..

D AUTHORIZED DEALER ONLY | Primary Dealer Code

Cheque Number

F E-payment only

Bank Name:..

Branch:..

Account Number:..

City/State:..

Stamp of Receiving Agent

E CBN USE ONLY

Amount Applied for N

Amount Allotted N

Under 'Allotment Preference,' you are to indicate if you prefer a paper certificate or an electronic one. Note that the paper option is no longer available. The custodian will issue you an investment letter in place of a printed certificate.

Under 'E-allotment Details,' you are to indicate your CSCS number. If you do not have one, your stockbroker will help you apply for one if you choose this option (which attracts no fees compared to a Custodian who charges a certain percentage of the amount invested). You should have all requirements in place before bidding; else, you may have no options.

Part B is where you fill in your details and sign your usual signature. It is also here that you indicate the bank account you want the bi-annual interest payment paid into. Note that the account name should be the same as the investor's name. If you are investing jointly with your spouse, the bank account has to be a joint account. If you are an individual, you are required to fill only section 1. You need to fill section 2 if it is a joint application, e.g., husband and wife.

A couple, investing as husband and wife, make it easy for one partner to have access to the investment if the other partner is unavailable for whatever reason. That is something you need to consider.

Corporate applicants like companies, agencies, and organizations are required to fill section 3.

Part C is for applicants who do not have a signature, to place a thumbprint, signed and dated by a witness who attests to the fact that the applicant has a clear understanding of what she is doing.

That's all. If you are outside Nigeria, the form can be sent to you electronically to print out, fill, sign, scan, and return by email as an attachment.

By Thursday afternoon, you will know if your bid was successful or not.

7: HOW TO BUY A NEWLY ISSUED FGN BONDS

In this chapter, we will walk through the process of subscribing to a newly issued Federal Government of Nigeria (FGN) bond. This is the initial public offering of bonds by the federal government to investors at face value or par value.

After the initial issue, the price of the bond goes up or down on the stock exchange or over-the-counter market based on market fundamentals, including demand and supply.

Participating in a primary bond auction allows investors to purchase bonds directly from the government at the initial issuance price (par value of N100) without the need to pay commissions and fees.

This is the cheapest way to invest in FGN Bonds. There are two main ways of buying a freshly issued bond.

A. SUBSCRIPTION BY AUCTION

This is an offer of fresh bonds to the investing public through an auction process. The auction works the same way as the reopened bond auction described in Chapters 5 and 6.

The Federal Government, through the DMO, sends out an Offer Circular, which contains details of the offer through regular channels - media and dealers.

Below is an Offer Circular for FGN Feb 2031 and FGN Feb 2034 (7 and 10-year tenor bonds).

DMO ♗ DMO ♗ DMO ♗ DMO ♗ DMO ♗ DMO ♗ DMO ♗ DMO ♗ DMO ♗ DMO ♗ DMO ♗ DMO ♗ DMO ♗ DMO ♗

OFFER CIRCULAR

DEBT MANAGEMENT OFFICE
NIGERIA

Pursuant to the Debt Management Office (Establishment) Act 2003 and the Local Loans
(Registered Stock and Securities) Act, CAP. L17, LFN 2004

DEBT MANAGEMENT OFFICE

on behalf of the

FEDERAL GOVERNMENT OF NIGERIA

Offers for Subscription by Auction

and is authorized to receive applications for

₦1,250,000,000,000.00 – FGN FEB 2031 (7-Yr NEW)*
₦1,250,000,000,000.00 – FGN FEB 2034 (10-Yr NEW)*

Auction Date:	February 19, 2024
Settlement Date:	February 21, 2024

SUMMARY OF THE OFFER

ISSUER:
Federal Government of Nigeria ("FGN").

UNITS OF SALE:
₦1,000 per unit subject to a minimum subscription of ₦50,001,000 and in multiples of ₦1,000 thereafter.

INTEREST RATE:
For **Re-openings** of previously issued bonds, (where the coupon is already set), successful bidders will pay a price corresponding to the yield-to-maturity bid that clears the volume being auctioned, plus any accrued interest on the instrument.

INTEREST PAYMENT:
Payable semi-annually.

REDEMPTION:
Bullet repayment on the maturity date.

STATUS:
1. Qualifies as securities in which trustees can invest under the Trustee Investment Act.
2. Qualifies as Government securities within the meaning of Company Income Tax Act ("CITA") and Personal Income Tax Act ("PITA") for Tax Exemption for Pension Funds amongst other investors.
3. Listed on the Nigerian Exchange Limited and FMDQ OTC Securities Exchange.
4. All FGN Bonds qualify as liquid assets for liquidity ratio calculation for banks.

SECURITY:
FGN Bonds are backed by the full faith and credit of the Federal Government of Nigeria and are charged upon the general assets of Nigeria.

INTERESTED INVESTORS SHOULD CONTACT OFFICES OF ANY OF THE FOLLOWING
PRIMARY DEALER MARKET MAKERS (PDMMs):

Access Bank Plc.
Citibank Nigeria Ltd.
Coronation Merchant Bank Ltd.
Ecobank Nigeria Ltd.
FBNQuest Merchant Bank Ltd.

First Bank of Nigeria Ltd.
First City Monument Bank Plc.
FSDH Merchant Bank Ltd.
Rand Merchant Bank Nigeria Ltd.
Guaranty Trust Bank Ltd.

Stanbic IBTC Bank Ltd.
Standard Chartered Bank Nigeria Ltd.
United Bank for Africa Plc.
Zenith Bank Plc.

* The DMO reserves the right to allot the FGN Bonds at its discretion.

DMO ♗ DMO ♗ DMO ♗ DMO ♗ DMO ♗ DMO ♗ DMO ♗ DMO ♗ DMO ♗ DMO ♗ DMO ♗ DMO ♗ DMO ♗

The Offer Circular usually contains the following information:

Name of Bond
Size of Offer
Auction and Settlement Date
Issuer
Units of Sale/Minimum Subsription
Primary Dealers etc.

Dealers send in client's bids before the advertised auction date.

B. OFFER FOR SUBSCRIPTION (FIXED COUPON)

The Federal Government also brings fresh fixed coupon bonds to the market to raise money for a specific purpose or project, often infrastructure related. The distinctive feature of this bond is that the coupon rate is fixed, and not determined by auction.

One example is the FGN Sukuk Bond issued to fund Federal Government road projects, offered at a fixed coupon rate of 15.75%.

Usually, a fresh bond offer is advertised in national publications both print and electronic. Here is an example of the FGN Sukuk Bond offer.

NOW OPEN- 10-YEARS FGN SUKUK BOND OFFER DUE 2033 AT 15.75% PER ANNUM

Dear Esteemed Investor,

We are pleased to inform you that the Debt Management Office (DMO) on behalf of the Federal Government will be issuing a 10-years FGN Sovereign Ijarah Sukuk Due 2033.

Sukuk are investment certificates or notes of equal value which evidence undivided interest and/or ownership of tangible assets or usufructs in compliance with Shari'ah principles. The Sukuk issuance will be managed by The FGN Roads Sukuk Company 1 PLC which is a special purpose vehicle set up by the federal government with the sole purpose of raising capital from the domestic capital markets to finance the development of road infrastructure in Nigeria.

Following its incorporation in 2017, the FGN Roads Sukuk Company 1 PLC has raised ₦200 billion (₦100 billion each in 2017 and 2018) from the domestic capital markets.

The subscription offer closes on **Wednesday October 11, 2023,** and the settlement date is **Friday October 13 2023** for the investing public.

See details of the Offer below:

Issuer	FGN Roads Sukuk Company 1 Plc on behalf of the Federal Government of Nigeria (FGN)
Instrument	Ijarah (Lease) Sukuk Due 2033
Tenor	10-years
Issue Size	₦150.0 billion
Unit of Issue	₦1,000 Per Unit
Minimum Subscription	₦10,000 (i.e. 10 units @₦1,000/unit) and in multiples of ₦1,000 (1 unit) thereafter
Rental Rate	15.75% per annum
Frequency of rental payment	Payable half yearly.
Use of Proceeds	Proceeds will be used solely for the construction and rehabilitation of key roads across the six geopolitical zones of the country.
Redemption	Bullet repayment at maturity
Security	Backed by the full faith and credit of the Federal Government of Nigeria.
Clearing System	CSCS
Listing	NSE and FMDQ
Paying Agent	Central Bank of Nigeria

To invest in the Sukuk bond, download the subscription form here.

For further enquiries, kindly reach:...

Let's explore the steps involved in subscribing to a newly issued

FGN bond using the above example:

STEP 1: REVIEW THE TERMS OF THE OFFER

The first step is to decide if the offer is for you. That starts with the minimum subscription required, if the coupon or rental rate and tenor works for you etc. The clearing system and listing is important. An NSE means the bond is tradable on the Nigerian Stock Exchange while an FMDQ listing means the bond is tradable on the over the counter market, which indicated the level of liquidity and a potential for profit if you desire to sell the bond before maturity.

STEP 2: OPEN AN ACCOUNT WITH A PRIMARY DEALER MARKET MAKER (PDMM) OR BROKER

If you do not currently have an account with any of the listed brokers for the offer, you need to open one. Before you do, find out if your bank or broker can submit an application on your behalf through a licensed broker (if they are not listed). If you are not sure, you can deal directly with brokers in the list.

Opening an account with a PDMM or broker typically involves providing identification documents, completing account opening forms, and funding your account with the required minimum amount.

STEP 3: PLACE YOUR BID

This involves filling the subscription form for the offer, which is obtainable via the broker on online from the DMO website. You will need an account with the CSCS which is the electronic central depository of financial instruments in Nigeria. Your broker can arrange to open one for you. You can also open an account with CSCS by filling the account opening form and providing the required ID documents.

Your broker will advise the cut-off date to submit their form so that they can collate the documents and submit before the offer closing date. Typically it is a day or two before the offer closing date.

Application must be accompanied with the full payment for the amount applied for. This means you have to fund your account with broker to cover you bid amount. There are no charges or fees to be paid by the investor.

There is coupon rate is as indicated, hence this is an application for subscription, not an auction per se.

STEP 4: WAIT FOR AUCTION RESULTS

After the bond subscription closes, the Debt Management Office (DMO) will review all submitted bids and determine the final allocation of bonds. Typically, results are announced the following day, and successful bidders are notified by their PDMM or broker. If your bid is successful, you will receive an allotment letter confirming the details of your investment.

You want to know if you were allocated the full amount you applied for. If the offering was oversubscribed as is often the case, the issuer often increases the amount based on their ability to utilize it.

In the case of the FGN Sukuk Bond 2023, the offer size was N150 billion while the total subscription was N652 billion, an oversubscription of 435%. The DMO allocated N350 billion from the amount, while N302 billion was returned to investors.

Typically, smaller investors get a full allocation while much bigger investors (e.g., institutional investors) get a pro-rated amount.

Subsequently, you will receive the bonds in your nominated account (S/4 or CSCS), ready for you to hold or trade as desired.

S/4 (Scripless Securities Settlement System) is the CBN system that helps in safekeeping, deposit and transfers, interest and principal processing, pledging of securities, issuance of the Government and CBN Securities in electronic form, auction processing, maintenance of all records for authorized transactions, and others.

STEP 5: MONITOR YOUR INVESTMENT

After receiving your bonds, it's essential to monitor your investment regularly. Keep track of coupon payments, maturity dates, and market conditions that may affect the value of your bonds. By staying informed, you can make informed decisions about holding or selling your bonds based on your investment goals and market outlook.

Subscribing to a newly issued FGN bond is a straightforward process that allows investors to participate in the government's debt issuance program. By following these steps and working with a trusted PDMM or broker, you can access the benefits of investing in FGN bonds and build a diversified investment portfolio aligned with your financial goals.

8: HOW TO BUY BONDS IN THE SECONDARY MARKET

The secondary market is the market for the trading of previously issued securities. You can carry out secondary market transactions in FGN Bonds through various platforms.

These include:

IN-HOUSE

Buying from another client within the same brokerage

NASD

Buying through the NASD (National Association of Securities Dealers) over the counter (OTC) securities exchange platform

FINANCIAL MARKETS DEALERS QUOTATION (FMDQ)

Bonds secondary market transactions are also transacted online over the counter using the FMDQ platform.

NIGERIAN STOCK EXCHANGE (NSE)

Bonds are also traded as securities in the Nigerian Stock Exchange through licensed stockbrokers.

All these transactions are executed through your broker . Bonds sold on the secondary market mainly come from two sources – individual and institutional (managed funds) investors. Minimum subscription varies from broker to broker based on their target client base.

If an investor aims to make a profit from the sale, they will not offer the bond at par value. The selling price is determined both by the market and individual seller. A cash-strapped investor may opt to drop his selling price to get a buyer faster.

Prices of bonds vary, and often it is cheaper to buy from the secondary market than through an auction. When your broker knows your budget and the maximum premium you are willing to pay (in a dropping rate scenario), she can advise you when a bond that meets your requirement shows up.

The same applies when rates are going up. You need to decide how much discount makes sense for you to take a lower coupon rate position. It is your call whether to buy or pass.

I will provide an illustration in Chapter 5 showing how a bond auction transaction works. The process is similar to buying in the secondary market. The main difference is that there is no auction.

The seller makes an offer, and you decide to take it or pass. In the Chapter 5 example (re-opening), the marginal rate amounted to a discount, since current market rates were higher than the coupon rate of the bond. That was the situation in 2017.

In this chapter, I will use the 2020 scenario whereby rates have dropped, and sellers offer bonds at a premium.

Mr. Bello wanted to buy N18 million worth of the 14.80% FGN Apr 2049 bond available for sale by his broker. The broker sends him the following quote:

Bond Type	14.8% FGN APR 2049
Settlement date	07-Jul-20
Maturity	26-Apr-49
Coupon	14.8000%
Yield (input)	10.55%
Frequency	2
Basis	1
Last coupon payment	26-Apr-20
Next coupon payment	26-Oct-20
Clean Price (solve)	138.180
Accrued interest	2.911475
Dirty Price	141.091475
Nominal Amount	18,000,000.00
Cash Amount	25,396,465.57

As explained earlier, the CBN issues all FGN bonds at the par value of N100. Due to dropping rates, the seller is offering the 14.80% coupon bond at 10.55%. That amounts to a unit value of N138.18 – a 38% markup on the issue price. The seller factors in his accrued interest, moving the price (dirty price) up to N141.09.

You will notice that this transaction was in July. Mr. Bello will not need to wait six months for his next coupon payment. It comes to him three months later in October (hence the dirty price).

Now to the crux of the matter: Mr. Bello has to shell out about N25.4 million to buy an N18 million bond. That is a premium of N7.4 million. That means his savings of N25.4 million drops to N18 million.

Mr. Bello has two options:

a) Proceed with the transaction and set aside part of the 14.80% biannual coupon payment to build back his capital.

b) Decline and look out for a bond with a lower premium.

As stated earlier, the only way to buy bonds at par value is during the initial issue. You will always have to deal with the issue of a premium or discount and make a decision on what works for you.

The price of bonds fluctuates continuously. Bonds put off many investors due to the long tenor. From the illustration above, there is a secondary market, and you can sell at a fair premium.

Bonds offer long-term financial stability. You don't have to return to the market, often looking for investment vehicles to put your money. You can simply buy a long-tenor bond and focus your attention elsewhere, doing other things with your time rather than continually watching market rates.

You need to be patient and look for a good entry so that you don't end up paying a hefty premium. Like in real estate, there is always more than one good deal in town. Don't feel pressured to close a deal if you don't feel comfortable with it.

A better deal will show up. Another new issue will come up. While waiting, you can park your funds in a money market instrument or fund with good returns.

Start small, gain knowledge and experience as you go along. Slow and steady wins the race.

9: HOW TO LIQUIDATE BOND BEFORE MATURITY

Holding long-tenor bonds is more advantageous than disadvantageous. You can sell your bond at any time, and liquidity in bond markets is growing. In this chapter, you are wearing the buyer's shoes. All you need to do is to tell your broker how many bonds you intend to offer for sale. The broker will handle the rest.

Your broker will advise the going price for your bond. You decide whether to go with the price or sell at a different price.

Based on the price, your broker will prepare a quote, as shown in the previous chapter. You get to see how much you will realize from the sale. You have an opportunity to proceed or pull out at any time before the deal is sealed (with money changing hands).

Your broker will get a buyer either from within the house or from other platforms (by posting your offer).

You can also sell through the stock market or over the counter market. In this case, you either advise your broker at what price to sell, or give her the go ahead to sell at the market rate. If you are not in a hurry to sell, you can wait till the market gets to your price.

We addressed the issue of why you want to buy bonds in the first place in Chapter 4. If you are buying bonds as part of your financial security plan, it does not make sense to liquidate before maturity. If you have a financial emergency, you can find other means of raising money to meet the need rather than degrading your financial security plan. If you are taking money away from bonds, you need to be sure where the money is going is secure and holds value long term.

Bond prices fluctuate in the secondary market but not as widely as stock prices do. There are three possible outcomes when selling your bond through the secondary market:

a) You sell at a premium (profit)
b) You sell at a discount (loss)
c) You break even.

You need to get your numbers right to know whether selling will work for you long term or simply hold to maturity.

As you gain more experience, you can buy and sell bonds for profit. The more you learn and do, the more options become available to you.

10: HOW TO BUILD UP YOUR CAPITAL INVESTING IN BONDS

One disadvantage of investing in bonds is the inability to roll over your interest and use compound interest to your advantage. If you buy a previously issued bond at a premium, there is the added disadvantage of capital depletion.

To build up your capital, you need to reinvest your earned interest. You need a certain level of discipline to execute this. If you consume your interest, compound interest cannot work for you.

You don't have that challenge if you have already built up your financial portfolio to the desired level, only living off the interest. Also, if you place your funds with a funds manager (e.g. mutual funds), they take responsibility for growing your funds, for which they charge a management fee.

If your funds are self-managed, there are ways you can reinvest your returns, especially if you have other sources of income to live on while you grow your portfolio.

You can do this by reinvesting your interest in the money market rather than leaving it where you end up spending it. You need to determine which money market instruments or platforms to invest the funds.

You have several options. These include:

- Treasury bills
- Commercial Papers
- Money market funds
- Fixed deposits

You can also borrow to invest.

It is interesting why this hardly occurs to many people. We borrow for all sorts of things except to grow our finances. You can grow your money faster by borrowing to invest if you know what you are doing.

Imagine you have access to single-digit loans (through your cooperatives, employer, etc.). Rather than borrowing to buy cars or household appliances, you can add the money to your funds and invest in new issue FGN bonds for double-digit returns.

For this to work, you must be able to repay the loan. That includes applying your coupon payments to the loan repayment.

In addition to growing your capital (buying more bonds than you would otherwise have been able to), the difference in rates between the loan and coupon becomes your profit.

Apart from making a profit, your more significant coupon payment speeds up the compounding process, enabling you to buy another bond (or money market instrument), moving faster towards your financial goal.

Your imagination limits your options. Whichever option works for you, you end up achieving your financial goals faster through the power of compounding.

11: LADDERING STRATEGY IN FGN BONDS INVESTING

In this chapter, we'll explore the laddering strategy—a popular technique used by investors to manage interest rate risk and optimize returns in bonds investing. Laddering involves spreading your investments across multiple bonds with staggered maturities, creating a "ladder" of bonds that mature at different intervals. Let's delve into the details of this strategy:

UNDERSTANDING THE LADDERING STRATEGY

The laddering strategy is based on the principle of diversification and risk management. By investing in bonds with varying maturities, investors can reduce the impact of interest rate fluctuations on their overall investment portfolio.

By buying bonds regularly, you get to take advantage of favourable rates to increase your yield, in addition to receiving more regular coupon payments as each comes due.

IMPLEMENTING THE LADDERING STRATEGY

To implement the laddering strategy in FGN bonds investing, follow these steps:

Take Advantage of New Offers: Subscribing to new offers allows you to buy bonds at par and commission free, and like an IPO, you can benefit from capital appreciation if the bond price goes up, increasing your portfolio value. It also presents an opportunity to sell. Having bonds with staggered maturities, ranging from short-term to long-term creates a ladder of bonds that mature at yearly intervals.

Purchase Bonds at Regular Intervals: Invest the allocated capital in FGN bonds at regular intervals, spreading out your purchases over time. For example, you may purchase bonds with shorter maturities initially and gradually extend the ladder by investing in bonds with longer maturities as they become available.

Reinvest Proceeds: As bonds in your ladder mature, reinvest the proceeds into new bonds with similar maturities, maintaining the structure of your ladder. This allows you to continually benefit from the compounding effect of interest income while ensuring a steady stream of cash flow from maturing bonds.

BENEFITS OF THE LADDERING STRATEGY

The laddering strategy offers several benefits for investors:

Risk Management: By diversifying across multiple maturities, investors reduce the impact of interest rate fluctuations on their portfolio.

Steady Cash Flow: The staggered maturities of bonds in the ladder provide a consistent stream of cash flow as bonds mature and are reinvested.

Flexibility: Laddering allows investors to adjust their portfolio's exposure to interest rate risk by fine-tuning the ladder's structure over time. You can sell some bonds and reinvest in better upcoming offers.

Optimized Returns: By investing in bonds with varying yields and maturities, investors can potentially achieve higher overall returns compared to investing in bonds with a single maturity.

The laddering strategy is a powerful tool for managing risk and optimizing returns in FGN bonds investing. By creating a diversified portfolio of bonds with staggered maturities, investors can achieve a balance between income generation, risk mitigation, and capital appreciation. Whether you're a conservative investor seeking stable income or a growth-oriented investor aiming for long-term returns, laddering can be tailored to suit your investment objectives and financial goals.

12: HEDGING AGAINST INFLATION WITH FGN EUROBONDS

In this chapter, we'll explore the concept of hedging against inflation using FGN Eurobonds. Inflation can erode the purchasing power of investors' funds over time, making it essential to employ strategies that preserve wealth and maintain returns in real terms. FGN Eurobonds offer a viable option for investors looking to hedge against inflationary pressures and exchange rate risks.

Let's delve into the details of this strategy:

UNDERSTANDING INFLATION HEDGING

Inflation hedging involves investing in assets that have the potential to maintain or increase in value over time, even in the face of rising inflation. These assets typically exhibit characteristics that allow them to outperform inflation, thereby preserving the real value of investors' capital.

FGN EUROBONDS AS AN INFLATION HEDGE

FGN Eurobonds are foreign currency-denominated bonds issued by the Nigerian government in international markets. These bonds are not affected by fluctuations in the domestic currency, making them an attractive option for investors seeking to hedge against inflation in Nigeria.

FGN Eurobonds are typically denominated in US dollars.

BENEFITS OF HEDGING WITH FGN EUROBONDS

Currency Diversification: FGN Eurobonds provide investors with exposure to foreign currencies, allowing them to diversify their currency risk away from the Nigerian Naira. Inflation in Nigeria may lead to currency depreciation, but holding Eurobonds denominated in stable foreign currencies can help mitigate this risk.

Preservation of Purchasing Power: By investing in FGN Eurobonds, investors can preserve the purchasing power of their funds in real terms. Even if inflation rises in Nigeria, the returns generated from Eurobonds in foreign currency may offset the erosion of purchasing power experienced in the domestic market.

Access to International Markets: FGN Eurobonds enable investors to access international capital markets and benefit from global investment opportunities. This diversification can enhance portfolio resilience and reduce dependence on domestic economic conditions.

Potential for Capital Appreciation: In addition to providing a hedge against inflation, FGN Eurobonds offer the potential for capital appreciation. Changes in interest rates and credit risk perceptions may impact bond prices, allowing investors to profit from market movements.

HOW TO BUY EUROBONDS

Investing in Eurobonds in Nigeria follows a similar process to that of ordinary FGN Bonds. Essentially, both FGN bonds and FGN Eurobonds can be acquired either through the primary market at the initial offering or through the secondary market for existing bonds.

The process involves completing the "Tender for Federal

Government of Nigeria Bonds" form, submitting it through any authorized dealer, and making the necessary payment upon a successful bid.

DEBT MANAGEMENT OFFICE
NIGERIA

NIGERIA'S EUROBONDS
CLOSING PRICES AND YIELDS
AS AT TUESDAY, FEBRUARY 06, 2024

Bond Name	7.625% US$1.118B NOV 2025 Eurobond	6.500% US$1.5BN NOV 2027 Eurobond	6.125% US$1.25BN SEP 2028 Eurobond	8.375% US$1.25BN MAR 2029 Eurobond	7.143% US$1.25B FEB 2030 Eurobond	8.747% US$1.0BN JAN 2031 Eurobond	7.875% US$1.5BN FEB 2032 Eurobond	7.375% US$1.5BN SEP 2033 Eurobond	7.696% US$1.25BN FEB 2038 Eurobond	7.625% US$1.5BN NOV 2047 Eurobond	9.248% US$750M JAN 2049 Eurobond	8.25% US$1.25BN SEP 2051 Eurobond
Price (US$)	98.101	90.957	87.643	94.493	87.739	93.520	87.487	83.389	79.997	76.736	89.462	80.371
Yield (%)	8.507	9.202	9.330	9.632	9.706	9.950	10.095	10.018	10.358	10.168	10.378	10.358
Yield at Issue (%)	7.625	6.500	6.125	8.375	7.143	8.747	7.875	7.375	7.696	7.625	9.248	8.250

Source: Bloomberg

Changes in global interest rates may impact the performance of FGN Eurobonds. Rising interest rates could lead to lower bond prices, affecting investors' returns.

Hedging against inflation with FGN Eurobonds can be an effective strategy for preserving wealth and maintaining purchasing power in the face of rising prices. By diversifying into foreign currency-denominated assets, investors can mitigate the impact of domestic inflationary pressures and benefit from international investment opportunities.

13: HOW TO INVEST IN BONDS WITH LOW FUNDS

Coming up with the minimum subscription amount for investing in reopened FGN bonds is a challenge for many who are just starting their investment journey. That should not stop you from moving ahead toward investing in bonds. You don't need N50 million to subscribe to initial FGN bond offers or buy from the secondary market.

If you find the minimum subscription demanded by brokers too steep for you, you can start with the FGN savings bonds. The minimum subscription is N5,000 and multiples of N1,000 after that. You have to locate a stockbroker whose minimum subscription works for you. Ask around colleagues who are active investors or know someone they trust.

You can carry out online research and contact them via contact phone numbers or emails provided. Again, what you are looking for is integrity and good customer service. CSCS domiciles FGN Savings bonds, so it doesn't matter which stockbroker you use as long as your stockbroker lodges your bonds with CSCS. You can confirm that by asking your broker for your CSCS account statement or checking directly on CSCS through your investor's account. The CSCS currently charges an annual access fee of N3,010 including VAT, for individual investors.

MANAGED FUNDS

Apart from investing directly through a broker, you have the option of investing in a money market fund whose portfolio includes bonds.

Investing in bonds through the primary auction is like buying wholesale. If you have challenges getting a financial institution with a minimum subscription that works for you, you can buy retail. You can invest indirectly by subscribing to money market funds which invest in bonds and accept minimum subscriptions that work for you. Some funds advertise as low as N2,000 and N5,000 monthly.

The advantage of subscribing to such funds is that they repackage different money market (wholesale) investments into in-house (retail) products which are more flexible. You can enter or exit within 24 hours since you are dealing directly with the broker. Some funds also generate monthly interest which you can opt to roll over to grow your capital or receive as monthly income. That means your money grows through your monthly payments and rolled-over interest, allowing compound interest to work for you at a faster rate.

With managed funds, your broker domiciles your funds. Hence you want to make sure you deal with a stable financial services company that will not go down with your money.

Make sure you investigate before investing to safeguard the return of your investment. Find out what you can about the company's financial health. Get a recommendation from friends, research online. You may be surprised at what you may find. If they have issues or are not doing a good job, one or two customers may have gone online to share their experiences.

Look at what the fund invests in and their track record. When you decide on the company to use, remain focused, and use their platform to build up your reserves to the desired goal. Despise not your seed, no matter how little it seems today. You will be amazed at how much you can achieve in years to come by making small monthly payments.

All you need is focus and discipline. Set clear financial goals and stick to it. If you save N5,000 per month for 12 months, you will have N60,000 at the end of the year, minus interest. That means in about 18 months, you would have crossed the N100,000 mark and ready to start fishing in the bigger waters. Eighteen months is not a very long time if you have long-term goals. It will only seem like a long time if you want instant gratification.

Your options are limited if you have low funds. It is in your interest to focus on saving up so that you have more opportunities to grow your money faster. That is why it is crucial to learn how to pay yourself first. Save first before spending and move your savings to where your hands cannot reach it – outside your bank accounts and into an investment working for you.

One thing that will help you is to continue investing in your financial education. Ask questions. The more questions you ask, the more answers you get. If you don't ask questions, you don't receive answers. The quality of the answers you get depends on the quality of questions you ask. The more you learn, the better questions you ask.

Keep your focus on your goal. Don't worry about how you will get there. Focus on what you need to do to take the next step. Few people believed when starting that they will get to where they are today. There is power in small steps compounded over time. Make each day and money that comes into your life count.

CONCLUSION

I hope this journey through the world of investing in FGN bonds has been enlightening and empowering. From understanding the basics of bond investment to exploring advanced strategies like laddering and hedging against inflation with FGN Eurobonds, we've covered a wide range of topics designed to equip you with the knowledge and tools needed to navigate the bond market confidently.

Whether you're a novice investor looking to start building your financial future or a seasoned investor seeking to optimize your portfolio, the benefits of investing in FGN bonds are clear. These bonds offer stability, attractive returns, and the flexibility to tailor your investment strategy to your specific goals and risk tolerance.

As you embark on your investment journey, remember that continuous learning and adaptation are key. Stay informed about market trends, reassess your financial goals regularly, and don't be afraid to seek guidance from financial experts when needed.

Above all, approach investing with patience, discipline, and a long-term perspective. Rome wasn't built in a day, and neither is a robust investment portfolio. By staying focused on your goals, remaining adaptable in the face of market fluctuations, and making informed decisions, you'll be well-positioned to achieve financial success and build a brighter future for yourself and your loved ones.

Thank you for joining me on this journey. May your

investments flourish, and may you reap the rewards of your diligence and foresight in the years to come.

ABOUT THE AUTHOR

Usiere Uko

Usiere Uko is a writer, speaker and business and finance coach. Aside from running other businesses, he is involved in helping entrepreneurs grow their businesses and attain their potential through a faith-based business academy and empowerment programs.

Originally trained as a Mechanical Engineer with extensive experience in the oil industry spanning design, construction, project management and organisational capability, his passion has been to educate people to achieve their fullest potential and live fully through acquiring skills (especially financial skills) to enable them to achieve freedom in other areas of their lives as an integrated whole.

Among the publications he has written for includes Punch (AM Business) and Daily Trust (SME Business) Newspapers, Leadership & Lifestyle and Today's Lifeline magazines.

Usiere is happily married with a lovely son and daughter.

BOOKS IN THIS SERIES

INVESTING IN NIGERIA

How To Invest In Nigerian Treasury Bills: A Beginner Guide To Fgn Fixed Income Investments

A Simple Guide To Investing In The Nigerian Money Market

BOOKS BY THIS AUTHOR

Practical Steps To Financial Freedom And Independence: Money Management Skills For Beginners

Before You Trade Forex: Things You Need To Know If You Desire To Start Trading Forex Profitably

Before You Invest In Cryptocurrency: A Simple Guide To Understanding The Cryptocurrency Market

101 Common Money Mistakes To Avoid: And How To Fix Them. Book 1: Expenses. Money Management, Making Your Budget Work

How To Avoid Living Under Financial Pressure: A Simple Guide To Getting Back Control Of Your Finances

Financial Independence For Employees: Making Your Job A Stepping Stone To Exiting The Rat Race

And Living Your Dreams

Managing Your Money Post Covid: Financial Management Skills For An Era Of High Inflation And Market Disruption

Retire On Your Own Terms: A Simple Guide To Financially Literate Retirement Planning

Your Ultimate Money Makeover: Manage Your Money Better, Take Control Of Your Finances And Your Life

Teaching Kids Money 101: Simple Parenting Strategies For Raising Financially Literate Kids From Toddler To Teen Years And Beyond

Uncle Ben's Money Lessons: Book I: Do You Want To Work For Money? A Vacation Story With An Adventure Into The World Of Money

Nft Investing 101: A Beginner's Guide To Collectible Digital Assets

Stock Market Investing 101: A Practical Beginners Guide To Online And Offline Stock Trading

Investing In Etfs 101: A Beginner's Guide For Building Wealth With Exchange-Traded Funds

Day Trading 101: A Complete Beginner's Guide To Trading The Markets

Forex Trading 101: A Beginner's Guide And Strategies To Profitable Currency Trading

Options Trading 101: A Beginner's Guide To Trading Stock Options

Futures Trading 101: A Step-By-Step Guide And Strategies For Beginner Traders

www.ingramcontent.com/pod-product-compliance
Lightning Source LLC
Chambersburg PA
CBHW072256310526
45795CB00012B/1669